Stepping Stones

(How To Become A More Affective

Stepparent)

Author

Marjorie A. Torchia

CRNP

1

contents

Section II

acknowledgment

This book is dedicated to my husband Michael, without whom

I would never have become a stepmother. He has always supported me, encouraged me and loved me. To my daughters, whose mothering I admire. And to my stepsons and foster sons, who opened their hearts to allow me a special place in their lives.

Copyright-2015

Publisher-Marjorie A. Torchia

Lancaster, PA

Printed in the United States of America

ISBN -13: 978-1508514930ISBN -10: 1508514933

foreword

Long ago, in a far away kingdom, there lived a girl named Cinderella. Cinderella was kind, smart and beautiful. When Cinderella was very young she had a happy life. Then one day her mother died. Soon after, Cinderella's father married a woman who had two daughters of her own. Cinderella's stepmother and stepsisters were not kind. The stepmother gave her daughters, Lottie and Dottie fancy dresses and wonderful toys. She gave Cinderella nothing. Then sadly Cinderella's father died too and Cinderella was left in the large house with her stepmother and Lottie and Dottie. Cinderella's life was awful.

The stepmother made Cinderella a servant in her own home. Cinderella had to rise early every morning and spend each day cooking meals, scrubbing floors, washing dishes and taking orders from Lottie and Dottie.

Does this sound familiar? This is historically the light in which a stepmother is cast. Why?

Step parenting is not a new phenomenon, it has been around since Old Testament times, Sara was a stepmother to Ishmael. Because Sara was unable conceive, and give her husband Abram a son, she had him sleep with her handmaiden who bore him a son. This led to jealousy and hatred so intense that Sara later sent the boy and his mother away. Her resentment towards the boy's mother and jealousy of her husband's son caused her to separate the father and the son. This scenario may not play out in the same way in today's world, but it's not far from what we see in our world today. The role of a stepparent is a growing one in our society due to the ever-increasing incidence of divorce and remarriage. About 50% of all marriages today are actually a remarriage for at least one of the adults. Sixty percent of divorced women and 75% of divorced men remarry within 10 years. Forty percent of remarriages involve children from a previous relationship. To top it all off, the divorce rate of re- marriages is higher than that for first marriages—reportedly around 60%!

When one partner brings a child or children into the new marriage the divorce rate is 65%.

When both partners bring children from previous relationships the divorce rate exceeds 70%! As of 2010 there were more blended families in America than any other type of family.

Given that 50% of all marriages end in divorce, a large percentage of the population is likely to become a stepparent, know a stepparent, or be in a relationship where one or both persons is a stepparent. We might say that we are facing a "Step-Parenting Epidemic" in our society. Yet, there is little information available to prepare us for the difficulties that arise in being a stepparent. There are innumerable books and parenting classes available that address the art of parenting our children and grandchildren—from the liberal child-rearing methods of "Spock" to the conservative child-rearing methods of "Dobson", but in light of the ever-growing number of stepparents, there is considerably less information available to prepare us for that role.

When we first become a mother or father an innate parenting instinct kicks in. There is no natural "step-parenting instinct", so even Mother Nature is no help. A new mother can always go to her own mother and get advice on parenting, but a new stepmother may not necessarily go to her mother, if her mother has not functioned in that role. Her mother may not have an understanding of the unique problems and issues confronting a stepparent.

Step parenting is a role that carries most, if not all, of the responsibilities and less of the rewards of parenting. A stepparent may do laundry, cooking, cleaning, and taxiing for a stepchild, or they may assume much, or all, of the financial burden of raising a stepchild. Yet as a stepparent there may be times when there is little or no acknowledgement or credit given for having made those sacrifices. Step parenting many times is a behind-the-scenes position, more of a supporting role. But a supporting role is a difficult role to fill for a lifetime. The biological parents are understandably the main characters in the child's life—as they should be. The stepparent role may not be the starring role, but it is a significant role just the same. This is not to say that there are never any rewards or moments of great satisfaction to be found in step parenting.

A stepparent can share in much of the joys of parenting, be involved in the making childhood memories and be part of living through many of the child's growing years experiences. Simply knowing that they played an important role in the child's life can bring much joy and satisfaction if they can keep a proper perspective of their role.

Your presence as a stepparent will be felt. It will have an impact. Whether the impact will be a positive or a negative one is up to you. If Cinderella's stepmother had such a profound negative influence on Cindy's life, couldn't she just as well have had a profound positive influence? Maybe Cinderella married the first prince that came along just to get out of the house and away from her stepmother!

A stepparent's reaction to their stepchild can create an environment where the parent-child relationship is not only preserved and cultivated following a divorce but an environment where that relationship can thrive. Or, the stepparent can prevent a relationship from existing altogether, as was the case in my own life. A stepparent can contribute to or cause the parent-child relationship to be totally nonexistent.

Imagine being in a position where you could potentially prevent a parent-child relationship from ever developing. That's power. A stepparent has a lot of power and will make a tremendous impact, which is why I would like to look at how we can make it a positive one.

As we have seen, historically the stepparent is often cast in a negative light. I can think of no story where the stepmother was "the kind one". We are all familiar with the story of Cinderella where the evil stepmother steals the father's affections from the child, takes her inheritance and banishes the princess to the cinder heap, treating her no better than a slave. This fairytale is a reflection of the bad image that stepmothers have today (Step parenting Myths).

Stepfathers are often portrayed as abusive and coldhearted. But thankfully in real life a stepparent can become a key figure in a child's life, leaving a permanent positive mark, as was the case with Douglas Gresham. He has written extensively about his stepfather, C.S.Lewis, the well-known author of The Chronicles of Narnia. He recounts his relationship with "Jack" and its evolution from stranger, to friend, to "much beloved step-father". How did Mr. Lewis accomplish this? In reading his stepson's writings you can see that he did it by becoming his friend. They spent much time together doing menial tasks. Douglas gained an appreciation for the beauty of nature and an understanding that all of the world's wisdom was to be found in books, from his stepfather. He describes him as being charming, kind and patient. C.S.Lewis gave himself totally to Douglas's mother and to Douglas and his brother in such an unselfish way that Douglas calls him a "veritable hero". He describes him as being a great scholar,

11

a great writer, a great teacher, a great theologian, and a great man. What an opinion to have come from a stepchild!

The ultimate example that we have of a near perfect stepfather is found in Joseph, the "stepfather" of Jesus. Joseph was the epitome of what a stepfather should be. He accepted Jesus as his own. He sacrificed his reputation, his job and his plans for what was best for Jesus and his mother. When he was confronted with Mary's pregnancy, before they were officially married, he accepted it. When Joseph was told to move his small family to Egypt to keep Jesus safe, he left his homeland and went to Egypt; later when he was commanded to move them back to Nazareth, he picked up and moved again, always doing what was best for his wife and child, a child that he did not father. Joseph took full responsibility and loved him as his own.

Chapter 1

Introduction

I do not consider myself an expert on step parenting and am not sure whether anyone could claim that title. My education, training, and experience on step parenting are both personal and professional.

My patents divorce when I was three. I had two stepfathers and one stepmother, all whom had an incredibly negative impact on my life. My first stepfather came into my life when I was only five years old and left when I was sixteen under disastrous circumstances. Those eleven years were significant years in my life. He was a career Navy man who was a strict disciplinarian and a violent alcoholic. There was no love, respect or even friendship between us, only fear. He ran our home in a military fashion and tried to demand our love. My stepmother was an insecure woman who could not separate her feelings towards the ex-wife (my mother) from her feelings for her stepchildren (my sister and me), to the degree that she prevented my father from every developing a close relationship with us. Even into adulthood, when my mother no longer had any influence, my stepmother's insecurities prevented my father from ever developing a relationship with me, my sister or our children.

Later in my life, I became the stepmother to four boys. This gave me a different perspective on step parenting—now as the stepparent rather than the child. As a result of my own negative experience I was determined to go about my own step-parenting role much differently. I wanted to have a healthy relationship with the boys. When they are grown, and I am gone I wanted to leave a positive legacy. When they looked back on our relationship I wanted it to be fondly. If they should ever find themselves in the situation where they may one day be a "stepparent" I want to be a positive role model for them to follow.

One of my own daughter's became a stepmother to two lovely girls. I watched as she struggled with the many obstacles that are inherent to step parenting.

In my professional life, I have been a Nurse Practitioner in Family Medicine for over 20 years, observing and interacting with patients and families who unfortunately had to confront the many difficulties that come with blending families. All that said, it is my hope that I have acquired some knowledge to impact those who find themselves in this difficult role.

My patients have often related stories that illustrate the negative impact stepparents have had on their lives and the lives of their children. A young professional woman—I've called her Kate—related to me that her mother died when she was 28 years old. Like many men, her father hated the idea of being alone and began dating within three months following her mother's death and soon remarried. Kate and her sister had family of their own. It didn't take long for Kate to notice that travel plans, holidays, and special occasions constantly centered on the new wife's children, to the exclusion of Kate and her sister's families. Kate believed that her new stepmother felt threatened by her and her sisters and their children. This behavior not only had an affect on one generation—Kate and her sisters—but the grandchildren as well. Kate and I discussed how much more affection and appreciation she would have felt for her stepmother if her stepmother would have included her father's children and grandchildren when making family plans.

The problem here does not rest with the stepmother alone. Kate would have a great deal more respect for her father if he would insist on spending more time with his own children and grandchildren. In this situation, the need to placate the second spouse is important to Kate's father in order to avoid problems in his second marriage, but that need is being met at the expense of several relationships, the relationship between Kate and her father and the relationship between her father and his grandchildren. Family dynamics never just affect one person.

My friend and patient—let's call her Nicole—had a mother who was remarried. The man was only a few years older than Nicole herself. Nicole always felt uncomfortable around her stepfather because he always offered nothing

16

but criticism of anyone she dated. Nicole eventually married, had a son and a daughter, later divorced and found herself raising two teens as a single mother. By the time Nicole was in her 40's her stepfather continued to degrade her and any man she became involved with.

As her own children grew up this man acted as if they were his grandchildren and constantly interfered with Nicole's parenting decisions.

He bribed Nicole's children by offering gifts and money then would use the bribes to exercise control over their lives. He gave Nicole's daughter a car with the understanding that she was to spend her weekends with him and Nicole's mother when she was home from college. He allowed Nicole's son to live with him and Nicole's mother (the boy's grandmother) and would give him money, but would completely control the boy's life.

As Nicole's stepfather, he should have had little or no control in her life or her children's lives. And yet, he constantly overstepped the boundaries. By allowing this behavior Nicole's mother was culpable as well.

Eventually, this completely eroded the relationship between Nicole and her mother. This man's need to control his wife, his stepdaughter (Nicole), and Nicole's children created turmoil in the entire family.

Deb, another adult child of a stepparent shared with me that she lived within three blocks of her father but never saw him due to the influence of her stepmother. Regardless of age we always have a need and a desire to have a relationship with our parents. A stepparent's influence does not only impact the life of the stepchild when they are young, but continues to influence long after the child grown. We all have a desire for relationship with our parents even as adults, therefore, a stepparent who interferes with that relationship has a lifelong impact. How much richer everyone's life would have been if Deb's stepmother would have put aside her own jealousy and insecurity and included Deb in their lives. Deb could have had a meaningful relationship with her father, as well as a friendship with her stepmother. It would have made holidays and life in general so much fuller.

Let's look at why these problems occurred, and how they can be avoided. How can the stepparent be a positive influence? How can we change the Cinderella story and all live happily ever after?

Parenting itself has been described as being a thankless job, if that is the case, this doesn't leave much hope for the job of step parenting. Step parenting is, to say the least, a difficult role and has some obvious disadvantages. I would suggest however that it also has its advantages. One being that it allows you to be invested in the child emotionally to a lesser degree than a natural parent. I care very much how my stepchildren ultimately turn out, but by not being the natural parent I'm not subject to the guilt most parents experience when their children make mistakes. Being a stepparent allows you to, in a sense, take a step back, be a bit detached, which is an advantage. It not only dissuades some of the guilt but it also allows you a little more objectivity.

Let me explain. I am so invested in the outcome of my biological children's lives that I cannot always be completely objective, I may be blinded by their shortcomings and may see attributes where there are none. Because I am their mother, they are a direct reflection of me, of my family and of my parenting skills. In contrast, as a stepparent my stepchildren are not a direct reflection of me; it's more of an indirect reflection.

A stepchild could not have inherited any traits from "my side of the family". This can be somewhat freeing. Through me, my daughter may exhibit traits of my grandmother but any similarity of my stepson to my grandfather is purely coincidental, I don't have to feel responsible.

He didn't get those from my side of the family!!!!

Chapter 2

Becoming a stepmother

Obviously I had been married before. My daughters were both out of college and already married when I met Michael. I came from a family of nothing but girls for 54 years: I had a sister, she had three daughters and I had two daughters. My daughter had two daughters (my youngest daughter has since had identical twin boys) and then I met and married a man who had four sons!

When I first met Michael his boys were 9-12-12-and 15 years old. When we were dating, Michael and I would often talk on the phone in the evenings. I sat in my quiet little house, alone, with just my dog, playing with a tennis ball. I would throw it down the hall from my bedroom and Lili would run after it for hours. Michael on the other hand had a fairly large home with four boys. The quiet, on my end of the phone—except for the occasional thump of the tennis ball and the subsequent running and sliding of my dog—was in great contrast to the chaos heard at the other end.

The music, the break dancing, the arguing, and the constant interruptions (every parent knows the only time your children actually want to speak with you is when you're on the phone), prompted Michael to ask me, "Are you sure you want to take on the work of raising four boys?" I responded, "Sure, what better use could I make of my life but to help you raise your four boys?" But he was correct, it was a lot to take on: Four boys to cook for, do laundry, and clean up after; four boys to get through the teen years; and four boys to pay for college educations.

At one point in our relationship Michael asked me if four boys were more work than two girls? I answered, "It's not more work, it's just different". "In what way", he asked. "Well let me tell you." I went on to explain to Michael that one day I was sitting very quietly in his van; the four boys were sitting behind me; and Michael had gotten out to pump gas. One of the twins announced, "I think I have to fart!" Of course coming from a family of girls, I was mortified. I explained to him that in our family that was the "F" word.

We didn't say it; we didn't talk about it; and we certainly didn't do it. Boys not only say it, they loudly announce it with pride, and then they try to do it on each other. That, I explained was the difference between boys and girls. What had I gotten myself into?

Along the way there arose two separate occasions where one of the boys brought home a "stray". Steve came after spending a week at the beach with us. His mother left him when he was a young boy and he had a difficult relationship with his alcoholic father. He was seventeen at the time, the same age as the twins which left me with three seventeen year-old boys in the house at one time! Steve lived with us for one year but now over ten years later we still fill the role of "parents" in his life.

A few years later, when one of Michael's boys was in college another young man, Lemuel who seemed to appear often in my kitchen and soon became a regular fixture for holidays, weekends and summers. He ended up being with us off and on for ten years until he married. To this day we still serve as substitute parents to him and his wife.

23

We have been together for over eighteen years now, and the boys are all in their early thirties. I've learned a lot about step parenting and about boys.

As I said, I do not claim to be an expert, but I have been a mother, a stepmother, a foster mother, a grandmother, and as a family practice Nurse Practitioner I have watched many couples encounter difficulties as they try to blend their families. I have learned about step parenting through my personal and professional journey and would like to provide some "Stepping-Stones" if you will, to being a more effective stepparent. Because I took on the role of a stepparent to boys ages 9-12-12-and 15, these suggestions may not apply in a situation where the stepparent has been a parent to the child from a very young age or if the natural parent is completely out of the child's life and the stepparent is the only parent they know. I believe these guidelines will help any stepparent in their journey in raising a stepchild.

Chapter 3

Stepping Stone #1-Do not try to become the other parent.

Understand that you never will be the other parent.
The last thing you ever want to hear from any stepchild is, "You're not my Mom!" (or Dad). So, from the very start make up your mind to never try to replace the other parent.

Your stepchildren have a mother and a father. The best you can hope for is to be their friend. You are in a unique position to be the pseudo-parent/friend to that child. No one else can do that. The child will have friends and they have parents, but who other than a stepparent can be both? Many stepparents try, in vain, to become the other parent. Some families even go so far as to require the child to call the stepparent "Mom or "Dad".

Since my parents divorced when I was only three and we moved far away from my hometown, I didn't have the opportunity to know my father, but I never thought of my stepfather as my father. He wasn't the best by any stretch of the imagination, but even if he had been, I don't think I would have ever thought of him as my father. Somehow in my little brain I held onto the knowledge that somewhere there was a man who was "my Dad".

Perhaps, in a situation where the other parent is deceased or completely out of the picture is it possible for a stepparent to be thought of as "the parent" and called Mom or Dad, but this is more often the exception rather than the rule. For example, I know a young man who married a young woman who had a child out of wedlock. The child's biological father was never in the picture. The child was only two when they married so the stepfather was the only father she ever knew. To her he was her "Daddy". But when the child's other parent is living and still in the picture, unless the child decides to call you "Mommy" or "Daddy" on his own, the title should not be forced on them. You cannot take the place of the natural parent, but by the same token no one can take your place either.

Whatever impact you have on that child's life is yours alone. Your relationship is exclusive to you. Just as you are not the mother, neither can the mother be the stepmother. Accept the role and enjoy it.

The pull to know our biological parents is very strong. We have all heard stories of the great lengths children who have been separated from their parents at birth have gone to reconnect with their biological mother and/or father.

Don't try to be "the real Mom" or "the real Dad". Those spots are taken. To tell a child that you, who up to this point were a total stranger to that child, are now going to be their "new Mommy of Daddy" is ludicrous. You may be Daddy's new wife or Mommy's new husband but you are not that child's new Mommy or Daddy. You are the child's new Step Mommy or Step Daddy. And that's OK. Carve out your own niche.

Chapter 4

Stepping Stone #2-Speak positively about the other parent.

When we have a brother, sister, Mom or Dad who exhibits negative traits, somehow it's OK if we comment about those traits, but we don't want anyone else to make such comments. A brother can call his sister a "jerk" but he'd better never hear it coming from anyone else!

Likewise, parents are people too, and they will naturally have negative traits, but a child does not want to hear about those traits from someone else, especially if that someone else is their stepparent. It is difficult for children to think of their parents as people. To a child the parents are just "Mom" and "Dad". As children grow older they will eventually begin to see their parents as individuals with both good and bad traits, this vision takes years to develop. Even after they see their parents as real people with real faults, they will still love them. It's difficult enough for a young adult to realize that Mom or Dad is not perfect, but do you really want to be the one who brings his to a child's attention?

As a stepparent you will obviously come to know the negative traits of your spouses' ex, and it may be very difficult to refrain from being critical, but it is important to refrain.

Speaking negatively about a child's parent puts the child in a precarious position because those negative comments challenge the child's loyalty. The child may not say anything, but they know when you are being critical, and being innately loyal to their parents, will not respect you in the end. Why put yourself on the enemy list by criticizing the child's mother or father?

If it is necessary to discuss something negative concerning the other parent, do it privately. If the divorce was a difficult one it should be kept between the adults. Children don't need all of the gory details. They can't understand it and shouldn't have to hear about it. So, if the divorce details need to be discussed don't do it in front of the children.

Try to discuss controversial subjects objectively instead of critically; the child can respect that. For example, if the other parent drinks alcohol with their teenage son, discuss the consequences of underage drinking rather than the fact that the other parent should not allow it. Discuss the subject not the person.

Let me give you an example of how I handled a touchy situation with one of my stepsons. Michael and I had a situation where his ex-spouse approached the issue of childhood responsibilities differently than the way we approached childhood responsibilities. Instead of criticizing her approach I waited for an opportunity to initiate a conversation with the boys about how families may have different attitudes regarding responsibility— some families taking a hard nose approach to teaching responsibility, others taking a soft-handed approach. I discussed the "subject" of responsibility objectively never mentioning their mother's name or how she chose to handle it. We talked about responsibility in general, without passing judgment as to whether their mother went about it rightly or wrongly. This gave the boys an opportunity to look at the situation objectively and decide for themselves how it should have been handled and how they may one day chose to handle the issue when they have children.

Some kids have chores and others don't. Some families have the children do the yard work while others may not. Some earn their allowance and others are just given an allowance. Which approach is good or bad, right or wrong, can be discussed in a general sense, noting the pros and cons without being critical of anyone. Approaching controversial issues in this manner develops a sense of respect for the stepparent simply because no one judged the other parent as being good or bad.

Chapter 5

Stepping Stone #3-Do not compete with the children for "position" in your spouse's life.

Since love truly has no limits, there's no need to attempt to position your self above or in front of the stepchildren. Love is endless. People, especially children have an unlimited capacity to love. No matter how much we may love one person, that love does not take love away from another. Therefore, you never have to compete with your stepchildren for a position in their parent's (your spouse's) life.

You are the natural parent's spouse; the children have a completely different relationship with their parents. You can never fill the same place in his/her heart that the children fill. So it's just not necessary to even try. A parent will love a child forever in a different way than they will love their spouse.

It is to be expected that as the children are growing up

they may need more of their parent's time and energy. after the job with the children is over you will still be there. You may have to forfeit some time now but it is a necessary loss if you marry someone with children.

Would you resent the time your husband spent with the children if they were your children? Time in the evening spent on homework, time watching their concerts or sporting events, and parent-teacher meetings are all time demands naturally placed on parents. It's part of being a family, even if it is a blended family.

Forfeiting some time with your spouse will be worth it in the end. He/she will be eternally grateful that you understood these demands on his/her time and he/she will love and respect you for making the sacrifice. Remember, it's his/her job to raise the children; it's not his/her job to raise you. In time, the children will also realize that you were not selfish with their parent's time and attention.

A few years ago I wrote a short story for my grandchildren to illustrate the point that love is truly limitless: 33

MAGIC PUDDING

" This was the second tooth Gracie had lost this week. " I guess the tooth fairy needs some more teeth", she thought. Aunt Shannon just had twin baby boys and I guess they were going to need some baby teeth soon. So Gracie tied the string around her front tooth and Mom pulled as hard as she could. POP, out flew the tooth! "Oh", said Gracie. It surprised her, but Mom was right; it didn't hurt; and it only bled a little bit. Now she could put this tooth under her pillow just like the last one and get some money for it. Maybe she would have enough to buy a new toy! But now that she was missing two of her front teeth it made it a little hard to eat. Mom said let's makes some magic pudding. Magic pudding! Gracie and her sister Elizabeth Anne had never heard of magic pudding. What kind of pudding was that? And what was in it? Well Mom said it has a little of this and a little of that and toss in a little love and its done.

So Gracie and Elizabeth and Alex, (Mom) went to the kitchen. They got out the bowls, the spoons, the mixer and

34

the pans and started cooking. Mom put in some sugar with a smile and Elizabeth added some vanilla with a kiss.

Gracie stirred in some chocolate with a hug and they baked it for an hour. It came out of the oven all hot and sweet, so Mom said let's invite some friends over to help us to eat our magic pudding. The girls still weren't sure what made it magic but they called their friends, Mary Margaret and her sister KK, their baby brother Ben, and they also called Miss Amy and told her to come over with her kids, Sam and his sister Caroline. Then they decided to call both of their Grandmothers and Grandfathers, Mimi, their cousins, aunts, uncles and neighbors.

Mom didn't know that the girls had invited everyone they knew to come over for some magic pudding. When everyone got there it was at least 100 people, and they all wanted to taste the pudding!!! Gracie and Elizabeth Anne realized that they only had one bowl of pudding but Mom said, " It will be alright, you'll see". The girls got out the bowls and spoons and started scooping out the pudding. Everyone formed a line and got a bowl.

They couldn't believe what was happening, the pudding bowl was never empty!! Their friends got some, Mimi, SueSue and Pop, Mom-Mom and NoNo, Poppie and Nina, Mom and Dad, even Mousse, Moose, Lili-girl, and Lily-dog and all of the puppies got some and there was enough for everyone. Finally when the last person in line got their bowl full of magic pudding the girls began to understand what made it magic? The pudding was made with LOVE, and just like love when you give some to someone there's still more to give to the next person and the next and the next. They never ran out and there was enough for everyone.

Your spouse's love for his children may rob you of some time and attention, but it does not rob you of love. We never run out of love, there is enough for everyone. Children never run out either. They have enough for their parents, their grandparents, their step-grandparents, their brothers and sisters, their step and half brothers and sisters and they may even have some left over for their stepparents.

Chapter 6

Stepping Stone #4-Leave the major disciplining to the "Real Parents".

The disciplining of children is a controversial subject to say the least. If you ask ten people's opinions on disciplining a child you'll get at least eleven answers. Disciplining a stepchild is an even more slippery slope. If you, as the stepparent take on the disciplining no matter how much you love those children, you are taking the chance of becoming "the bad guy"—a role the stepparent wants to avoid. One of the last things a stepparent wants to hear is, " I don't have to listen to you, you're not my Mom/Dad". At the same time, the child does need to understand that you are an adult, and a parental figure in their life. That role entitles you to a certain amount of respect. The problem is that being an adult, parental figure while at the same time not being the "real parent" and trying to avoid being the bad guy is like walking a tightrope.

As an adult who is assuming a parental role in the home, your thoughts concerning discipline should be expressed and seriously considered by your spouse. Discipline styles vary, and issues such as paddling always need to be discussed and agreed upon by the natural parents. It would be very helpful if the biological parent were to communicate to the child what is expected of him when the stepparent is in charge. But given the pain involved in a divorce and the variety of feelings when an ex-spouse remarries, it may be a lot to ask of the ex-spouse to be an advocate for the stepparent. However, it would be the optimal situation if all of the adults involved could put their feelings aside and work together for the good of the children.

The stepparent has a vested interest in the children and the behavior of the children affects everyone in the home. However, the final decision regarding the discipline should ultimately rest with the biological parents. In situations that involve serious discipline or when determining some of the rules of childrearing such as which movies they may watch or how to deal with lying, there is no reason why your spouse shouldn't be able to discuss this with "the other parent". If possible, that needs to be facilitated.

In my experience as a stepparent there were times when I would have handled certain situations differently with my stepsons if they had been my sons. For example, one of my stepson's had the responsibility of taking out the trash every Thursday night and carrying it down to the bottom of our very long driveway. At 23-years old I was surprised to see how often he needed to be reminded about the chore and frustrated to see my husband decide that it was easier to carry it down himself rather than to go into the "trash lecture" again.

Had he been my "son" he would have woken up with the trash bag on his bed each week until he could remember to do that chore. Can you imagine how I would have been received if, as the stepmother, I put the trash bag on his bed or even been the one to lecture him about the trash? Bottom line is, he's not my son, and putting up with constant trash reminders by my husband, or watching my husband deal with the trash himself, was worth not alienating myself from my stepson.

Discipline is a "no win" situation for a stepparent. If I disagree with my husband and nag him to take some action to teach his son to be responsible, then he becomes angry with me.

If I nag my stepson to be more responsible with the trash then I become the "bad guy". Taking it upon myself to handle the situation by placing the trash bag on his bed puts my husband in a difficult position. Since he does not agree with me about the seriousness of the infraction or the steps taken to correct it puts us immediately at odds. There are better approaches a stepparent can use in these situations.

Unfortunately "normal" parental behavior such as putting the trash bag on the bed, yelling, nagging, demanding, lecturing, or instilling guilt are not well received from a stepparent. Like it or not stepparents are held to a different standard.

Chores are often a point of contention in any household. It should be explained to children that chores are a part of sharing the responsibilities of being a family. Everyone has the privilege of living in the house and eating the food therefore everyone should share in the work of maintaining it. Personal responsibility in caring for our own things as well as respecting the family as a whole by not expecting others to live with your mess is something we all need to learn and teach our children. These issues should be discussed as a family, without animosity or anger and the consequences of not sharing in the responsibility should be laid out. Consistent defiance to the house rules would have to be dealt with. The parent and stepparent may agree together on the rules and the punishment but it may go a little smoother if the natural parent is the one to dole out the punishment.

If the stepmother is home with the children and responsible for the home the majority of the time she may have to address an issue such as an unclean room or clothing lying around the house by reminding the child of the expectations and the possible consequences of disobedience.

This does not have to be done with an attitude or anger, just the facts. Then if the child continues to ignore the reminders the natural parent may need to step in and enforce the punishment. The stepparent can even become an ally; by reminding the child "You may want to spend some time cleaning up your room tomorrow so that you don't get into trouble". Or, "Remember today is trash day". You're not acting as the enforcer just as the reminder, to help them avoid punishment. This is much better for every one. Rather than being the one who says, "You haven't done your chores this week so there will be no movie with your friends on Saturday".

I found it very interesting that when my husband and I opened our home on two separate occasions to young men who needed a place to stay, basically becoming their foster parents, disciplining them was not as much of an issue. The first was when Michael's twins were 17 and a friend of theirs whose mother had left when he was a child and who had a difficult relationship with his father, needed a place to live. We agreed to have Steve live with us. A few years later when one of Michael's twins was in college he brought home a young man by the name of Lemuel who did not have a stable home and was putting himself through college. Lemuel stayed with us most weekends, summers and holidays. My role with these boys was a mother's role, but not a stepmother's. I cooked and cleaned for them but I wasn't married to their fathers. I found it interesting that I was much more able to discipline those boys than I was my stepsons. I could look at either Steve or Lemuel and say, "No, you're not ruining your dinner by eating cereal now". This is something I wouldn't say to my stepsons. It's difficult to explain why there was a difference but there was. These boys both had a mother, even if she wasn't acting at the time as their mother, so I was filling that role. I wasn't married to their fathers. As a matter of fact I didn't even know their fathers. Initially I was basically a stranger to both of them. Yet I felt more able to take on the role of a mother to them then I did with

43

my stepsons. To this day I still admonish them and advise them, but I have never felt the need to worry about them resenting me. I think this may have been because they both knew that I opened my home to them and did the motherly duties completely by choice, as I did with my stepsons. There was no other reason for Steve and Lemuel to be there other than that I wanted them there. They knew that they were not thrust upon me because I married their father. This was something that I never wanted my stepsons to consider.

I hope I have been able to convey the message to my stepsons that I chose to be their stepmother as much as I chose to be Michael's wife. They weren't added baggage that I had to deal with. I knew what I was getting in the deal and wanted it. Just as much as I chose to be a mother figure to Steve and Lemuel, I chose to be a stepmother to Paul, Matt, Chris and Andy. How great would that be for a child to be told by a soon-to-be step parent that they are as excited to become their new stepparent as they are about becoming a new wife or husband.

What about those situations where the stepparent must assume the role of the disciplinarian, when the need to discipline is immediate and unavoidable.

If a child is being willfully disobedient and disrespectful, you must act. If a child were to lash out verbally or physically then you must deal with the situation then and there.

Realistically you cannot wait until your spouse "gets home". A possible approach would be to treat the child in the same way that you would treat another person's child in that instance. Try to imagine that you are watching your best friend's child for the weekend. When you asked the child to clean up a mess that they had made the child says, "No, I don't have to listen to you". You may say, "I have asked you to clean it up and if you don't you will have to sit on that chair until you do". If they were verbally disrespectful you would make them apologize and maybe put them in a "time out". Just because he or she is not your child, if you are responsible for them at that particular time, you would deal with it as you felt any adult would, and later explain and discuss it with your friend. Just because it's not your child you wouldn't let bad behavior go unpunished. When backed into an immediate situation it may help to deal with the child in a very similar way that you would if it were the child of a friend. Actually he/she is, it's your best friend's child, your spouse's.

I often would be in the kitchen cooking and the boys would sit at the breakfast bar and discuss any number of topics with me. From faith to sex, to what I thought their future wives would be like, we talked. It gave me numerous opportunities to impress upon them my thoughts, my values and my opinions without putting myself in the role of the lecturing parent.

I had a situation with one of my stepsons, Chris. Instead of appreciating something I regularly did for him, Chris was developing an attitude of entitlement rather than appreciation and he was becoming a little disrespectful.

Chris has a very dry sense of humor and often teased me about how the woman's place was in the kitchen. One day when I was in the living room he asked me," Does Dad know you're out of the kitchen?" His comments were intended to be funny but I often told him he was going to have to be careful with that sense of humor.

I always kept a pitcher of homemade iced tea in the refrigerator, which all the boys loved, but seeing one day that the iced tea pitcher was empty my stepson took things a bit too far and said—in a not so nice tone of voice— "You'd better get in there and make me some more iced tea". I said, "Excuse me?" And he repeated the comment in the same tone of voice. So I made a fresh pitcher of iced tea and put it in the refrigerator with a big sign that read "NO TEA FOR CHRIS". When he inquired about the sign I said, "let me ask you a question. If you cut an elderly neighbor's lawn each week just to be nice to him and one day he came up to you and said, "Hey boy, the lawn needs cut; you'd better get right on that', how do you think you would feel? Instead of it being something you did willingly and that was appreciated, cutting the lawn was now demanded and expected.

47

I think you owe me an apology". He did apologize and I immediately went to the refrigerator and got him a big glass of iced tea and served it to him with a smile. I discussed the situation with a kind and practical response- no yelling or crying. It was a teachable moment without my being emotional and sensitive. I appealed to his "normal human decency". Don't bite the hand that feeds you! I can accept Chris' dry sense of humor, but when he stepped over the line and used his humor to make a demand, I withdrew the privilege of having iced tea. He never demanded any thing from me again, but he still teases me about a woman's place being in the kitchen. Great kid great sense of humor, great lesson.

Chapter 7

Stepping Stone #5-Recognize the uniqueness of relationships.

Each relationship is unique. The relationships we have with each of our children are unique and will greatly depend upon your gender and their gender, personality, and age. It will also depend upon our role of parent or stepparent, son or daughter. Combining all of these factors simply means that no two relationships are alike. We seem to accept differences in relationships among our friends, but somehow when it comes to our children, or stepchildren, we think that we should have the same closeness, and understanding with each of them. It won't happen. Children are individuals, and just like all individuals they have their own personality, which becomes known not long after birth and continues to develop along the way. Because of our individual personalities we will naturally connect and/or conflict with others and their individual personalities.

If you have conflict with a child/stepchild it just may be due to your personalities. Don't assume that the difficulties are due to the other parent trying to turn them against you, or that they are somehow undermining you.

Relationships are unique, but there are some common bonds that exist within those relationships; i.e. between a mother and a son, a father and a son, a father and a daughter and a mother and a daughter. As a stepparent understanding these common bonds will help you not to see yourself as the determining factor in the parent/child relationship. You have a tremendous influence over these relationships and you want it to be a positive one but you are not the only ingredient.

Mother-Son: a boy will often have a special bond and be very protective of his mother. If, as a stepmother you notice this protective bond, realize that it is not an assault on you. You are not his mother, and he will not have the same protective feelings towards you. That doesn't mean that you can't have your own great relationship with him.

As a stepfather, think about how you feel about your own mother. There is no need to compete to be your wife's protector.

Father-son: a boy's father is his role model of how to parent and how to be a man. Boys naturally seek the approval of their father but may not need to seek the same level of approval from a stepfather. It is not a rejection of you. It will help you, the stepfather to understand your stepson's need for his father's approval, and if possible, help him to gain it. You are actually taking on the role of another man in a boy's life who can mentor and teach him how to be an honorable man. In the father-son relationship, as a stepmother you need to allow your husband to spend the time and attention that he needs to spend in order to teach his son how to be a man. Respecting your husband and encouraging your stepson to appreciate all that he can learn from his father.

Father-daughter: a daughter often feels a special bond with her father. Many little girls go through a phase where they say they're going to marry their father.

His role and relationship with her is often a powerful influence over the type of man she ultimately marries. A daughter likes to please her father. She wants him to be proud of her. She feels safe with a father in her life and does not want anything to threaten this relationship. Daughters will guard and protect this relationship, and as stepmother you need to recognize that this bond is very natural and you should not compete or disrupt it. There is no place for jealousy, after all; you have a father, let her have hers. I think it would be very difficult to be the new woman in a girl's father's life, as well as a new man in a boy's mother's life. I counted myself somewhat lucky that my husband didn't have a daughter. But, if he had, I hope that I would not have felt the need to compete As the stepfather to a girl, you can have a loving relationship with her but it does not preclude her from loving her father as well. The importance of your role as a stepfather includes modeling in your marriage to her mother what a healthy man/woman relationship looks like. Your job is to be the kind of husband to her mother that you would want her to seek for herself.   52

Mother-daughter: a daughter will often try to be like her mother. Just as a son wants his father's approval, a daughter wants her mother's approval and may emulate her. If her mother is in the picture she is her role model, even if *you* feel that she is a poor one. A daughter may look to her mother as an example for fashion, interests and behavior.

If the real mother wears her hair short and is interested in sports the daughter may imitate her. As a stepmother, you may feel at times as if you are living with a miniature version of your spouse's ex-wife. If you have different interests you're going to have to understand that you will have a certain influence in your stepdaughter's life as she watches you but her mother is her main role model. If she comes home looking like a smaller version of your husband's ex-wife, keep it in perspective. You can't expect that influence not to exist just because the parents are no longer together.

Just as boys are protective of their mothers and seek their father's approval and girls go to a father for protection and want their mother's approval, it is also natural, at a certain age, for sons to compete with their fathers and girls with their mothers.

If as a stepparent, you observe this in the relationship don't exploit it.   Often in the teen years the natural parent/child relationship can become competitive. As a stepparent if you observe a conflict between a stepchild and the "other parent" don't malign them.   Don't encourage "sides" or point out things that will only hurt the natural parents relationship with their child. Don't see it as an opportunity to strengthen your own standing with the child.   As they mature and grow out of the rebellious/competitive stage it will only serve to hurt your relationship with them in the long run. Your job is to encourage respect, honesty, and love in all the child's relationships.

Be understanding of the natural tendencies that go along with gender and relationship.

If your stepchild's behavior falls in line with his or her natural tendency, don't take the behavior personally or take advantage of it. When you sense conflict, before reacting to your stepchild's behavior ask yourself if that conflict arises from your stepchild's nature as a boy or girl relating to their mother or father or if the conflict does truly involve you. If you have become the source of the conflict between the parent and the child, fix it.

As a mother I can say that I love my children equally but differently. They are different people; therefore our relationship will automatically be different. I think my younger daughter is finding this out already with her twins. They have different personalities, but she will love them both equally, just differently. In other words relax; relationships are complicated. Natural tendencies are the same the world over and each of our relationships are unique. And that includes yours with your stepchild.

Chapter 8

Stepping Stone #6-Do not take your frustrations with the ex-spouse out on the children.

Children are the victims in a divorce. Unfortunately the relationship between ex's is often strained. Ex-spouses often make each other's lives difficult to say the least. Do not discuss the issues with the children that should be kept between the adults. If your spouse's-ex has angered or frustrated you over issues such as money or schedules, do not pour out your frustrations on the children. They can't change what happened and they shouldn't have to hear about it, especially from the stepparent.

If your spouse's ex has messed with the visitation schedules and ignored previously planned holiday agreements, remember this is not the child's fault. Most of the time the children are not only unaware of agreed upon times, they are powerless to get themselves somewhere on their own. They may show up at your house 10 minutes before you were mean to go somewhere and have had neither a bath nor dinner.

If the other parent chooses not to take the high road in these situations, it can create havoc in your life, but always remember not to take it out on the kids. As children get older they may become more aware of difficult situation but are powerless to change it. Children cannot think ahead and consider what the plans are. Children cannot make sure they have eaten, had a bath and have homework done before returning to the other house. Realizing what has happened, they are probably embarrassed by the situation (unless they are extremely young at the time). Kids are smart, and figure out what's going on pretty quickly but are not in a position to change it. Think about how you would feel if you were put into a situation where you realize that you unknowingly have put someone out but do not have the power to change it. Even older children who realize that a difficult situation is arising because they were to be "out of Dad's and at Mom's by six", may find it difficult to control.

Along with time, money is another area where the child has no control. A child doesn't need to hear that "Mom" or "Dad" didn't pay a certain bill or "send the check".

When frustrations or irritating situations arise keep it between the adults, preferably between the parents themselves. They are the only ones responsible or to blame.

It is unrealistic to expect no conflict and frustration in a divorce. As the new partner it is very important for you to be accepted and even loved by your partner's children. But as is often the case in most of life's difficult situations, when a conflict arises it helps to place your self in the other person's shoes. Try, if you can, to imagine how threatened you might feel as the other parent. Put yourself into the position of a mother who now has to share her children with her ex-husband and his new spouse. The kids may think that the new step Mom is great. She's new and fun and does everything she can to get them to like her.

That's hard to compete with. Because of course, Mom has rule and is no fun at all. Now every other weekend the kids can't wait to go to Dad's. Mom may have to miss out on special occasions like first dates, proms or being there when the child comes home with his driver's license, depending on which weekend it falls on. As the stepparent, try to be sensitive to how the other parent may be feeling. It won't kill you to share special occasions with the other parent. Invite them to be present to take prom pictures or encourage your spouse to share the fun times. If one parent took the child to get his/her permit let the other parent take him/her for his license. You are all in a parenting role, which means you all should be involved in the good times and the bad. As the spouse to one of the parents you have the opportunity to openly discuss these things with your spouse and help them to see areas and times when they can be fair. I do understand that this is asking a lot, especially if you are being portrayed as the "bad guy" by the ex-spouse. Do it anyway, be sensitive, it's just the right thing to do.

Chapter 9

Stepping Stone #7-Be aware and understanding of mixed messages.

The rules and lifestyle in one home may be drastically different from the rules and lifestyle in the other home. Some homes are run on a schedule, with set bedtimes and mealtimes while others are run in a more relaxed style without schedules. Some people are comfortable in chaos while others need order. Can you imagine how confusing it is for a child who may spend two or three days in one type of environment and the rest of the week in another?

This is not a unique situation with separated or divorced couples. It has been said that opposites attract. When couples first marry they may feel that the differences between them compliment each other, but when the marriage ends in divorce, their differences often become points of contention. Two people who have very different ideas on how things should be done can become the parents of the same children who end up living in two drastically different homes.

Here are these poor kids who—on Monday night—eat dinner at 8:00 o'clock and go to bed whenever they wish, while on Tuesday they eat dinner exactly at 6:00 o'clock and are in bed by 9:00. The bowl of cereal they routinely eat at 5:30 at Mom's house—to hold them off till their 8:00 o'clock dinner—does not go over too well at Dad's house when dinner is served at 6:00.

If a child can't see the floor of their room for the piles of clothes at one parent's house but had better hang up their coat as soon as they walk in the door at the other's, you can see how it could get a little confusing for the child.

We haven't even mentioned issues that involve differences in morality, belief systems and philosophies of life: One parent allows the children to watch PG-13 movies and believes that drinking alcohol at home at age seventeen is OK, vs. the other, who permits only G-movies and forbids drinking in the home.

How about when one parent's priority is that life should be about fun and family while the other professes the virtues of work and striving to reach one's potential?

You may not be able to prevent conflicting messages due to personal differences but you need to understand that the child is receiving them. As the stepparent you have the luxury of being able to take a step-back, evaluate the situation, and try to look at life through the child's eyes. As difficult as it may be, remember that just as you and your spouse deserve the right to maintain the values you establish in your home, the other parent has just as much right to run their home as they please. How difficult and confusing it must be to a child living with such inconsistency.

If the child is struggling with extreme differences and you find out the other parent let them do something you would not have permitted, don't blame the child. Talk to your spouse about it and them help them as they talk to the children about it.

Yes, they need to follow the rules of your home, but keep things in perspective. You only have control of what takes place under your roof and on your watch. We never have control over another person's actions, even though it might affect the children. Divorce means that you no longer have a say in what the other parent does. The best-case scenario is when parents can agree to rules that are best for the child but obviously this will not always happen because to compromise to some may mean defeat.

As a stepparent don't let these differences in lifestyles cause conflict between you and your spouse. Don't give off unspoken attitudes of anger, resentment or disapproval to the children. Be flexible and understanding when the differences in parenting methods cause inconveniences to your schedule and life.

Chapter 10

Stepping Stone #8-LOVE. Love your stepchildren like your own.

The Bible says that love is patient; love is kind; it does not envy; it does not boast; it is not proud. It is not rude; it is not self-seeking; it is not easily angered; it keeps no record of wrongs. Love does not delight in evil but rejoices with the truth. It always protects, always trusts, always hopes, always perseveres. Love never fails (1 Corinthians 13: 4-8).

These qualities of love are displayed in a blended home by treating children—whether they are "yours, mine or ours"— with equal patience, kindness, selflessness, trust, protection, hope, perseverance, and love. You can love all the children in your home by providing equal time, attention, money, respect, and consideration. Your stepchildren deserve the same benefit of the doubt and the same allowances you would make for your biological children.

Equal time is tricky. When an intact family lives under one roof all family time is spent together. When your children now live under two separate roofs and parents have to share the time with the children, often with one parent given less time, this becomes difficult and creates resentment. The parent, your spouse, feels the pressure to make their time with their children "quality time". When we live as one family, there are times when we give little thought to the quality of our time with our children.

This pressure combined with the guilt that often goes with putting children into a divorce situation may cause some parents to overcompensate by trying to make every minute count. If other children and a second wife now exist, this creates conflict on how time will be divided. The parent will feel torn, there's only so much time in a day. How can they make things equal when they constantly feel that they have something to make up for?

As the new spouse, and the stepparent, there will be times when you feel like the outsider. Times when your spouse may want or need to spend time alone with his/her children. You don't need to feel threatened or put out.

If this were a first marriage and these were your children together there would be times when your spouse would engage in activities with the children without you, and you wouldn't feel threatened or jealous. You would probably enjoy the break. If your spouse took the children to a soccer game or to the movies you would enjoy the free time. Why should you feel jealous or resentful because your spouse is spending time with your stepchildren?

Understand that your spouse may at times be torn between his/her biological children to his/her first spouse, his second child or children (with you), you, work, church and everything else that pulls at them.

This conflict of how to spend time can also occur with money. As I previously related, my husband made it clear that he had the responsibility to put four boys through college. This was obviously going to be a significant expense. We managed our finances together; there was no yours or mine. If they had been our children together we would have had this expense, so what's the difference.

This approach works well whether we are dealing with money, time or attention. Think of it as if this were your natural family, with no other "parent" involved, what would take to raise these children? If your wife spent a certain amount of money for school clothes or spent four hours a week with her child as a Girl Scout leader (your stepchild), it should be no different if it were your natural child. Don't resent the time or money spent. Think of yourselves as one family unit.

Along with feeling love for your stepchildren we have to learn how to appropriately express love to them. I love my stepsons but I made a mistake early on, I did not openly show them affection. My nature is more reserved, and my way of showing them love was more about my doing for them rather than being physically affectionate towards them. From the time that Michael and I started dating if I heard one of the boys mention that they needed something in particular I would get it, and within a day it would just be there. One time I heard one of them say that he needed "grip tape" for his skateboard. I didn't even know what "grip tape" was but within 24 hours I found out, bought it and had it sitting on the table. It was my way of showing love.

Since my stepsons were so young when their parents divorced, being sons they naturally felt very protective of their mother. I feared that if I hugged and kissed them they would somehow feel that they were being disloyal to their mother. So I didn't. As they have gotten older they have actually become much better at showing me affection and I them, which I really appreciate. As they become adults they are able to handle any misguided guilt that they are somehow betraying their mother by caring about me. As adults they understand that loving one person does not take love away from another. I think we should love our stepchildren as if they were our own and discipline them as if they were someone else's.

I have heard it said that the best way to love your children is to love your spouse. Therefore, another way to love your stepchildren is to love your spouse. The health of the marriage relationship is important to all of the children. These children don't need another divorce in their lives.

Even though their parents are no longer together, they still need the security of knowing that the family as it has evolved is secure. Unfortunately children of divorce have learned the lesson that marriage may not be a forever thing.

Children from unbroken homes will still have this dream, children from broken homes know better. Since they now have this knowledge, I think it is important to give them a sense of security that your marriage is secure and that they need not worry that the rug is going to be pulled out from under them again. The strength of the marriage is important for the children but it is also important for your sake as well. Long after the children are grown and gone, the two of you will still be there, together. No one needs a second divorce.

Chapter 11

Stepping Stone #9- Remain in the background—take the supporting role—on the important days in a stepchild's life.

There are situations when your step child's biological parents hold a position of privilege, and as a stepparent, you must recognize such occasions, be quick to take a backseat and be patient until that time passes. For example, a stepmother may not have the privilege of helping to pick out a wedding gown or plan a wedding for her stepdaughter. Likewise, a stepfather may not have the privilege of walking his stepdaughter down the isle on her wedding day. Taking the backseat does not mean that you are any less proud or feel any less joy for your stepchild. Taking the backseat simply says that you recognize and respect the position each biological parent holds in your stepchild's life, and regardless of the time, energy, effort, love, blood, sweat, and tears that you may have put into the raising of your stepchild, there are events, celebrations, graduations, weddings, and even tragedies of illness and accident during which you must yield to the position held by the biological parent.

These days or times are not about you and you need to accept that fact. You may be just as proud, just as happy, or just as worried, but you are not the biological Mom or Dad. By the same token, you are not "a nobody" and you do have a role to play. You are the support for your spouse; you are the hoop under the skirt; the support beam under the floor; and that's an O.K. place to be. But the hoop under the skirt and the beam under the floor are not seen. These supports are important and respectable; but not always visible. Stay in the background; let the biological parents take their God given positions and fulfill their duties.

Chapter 12

Stepping Stone #10- Be the best stepparent this world has ever seen.

If you have children of your own, when they were born, in your heart you made the decision to be the best Mom or Dad this world's ever seen. I know I did. Of course I probably was not the best parent this world has ever seen, but I sure gave it my best. There is no perfect parent, no perfect child, or perfect marriage. There is no perfect stepparent, but we have to strive for that perfection.

Going into a second marriage with children involved is so different from a first marriage where you and your spouse had only each other to think about. Bringing children into a second marriage means it's not just about you and your spouse from the start. There are children involved who need to be considered. It's about so much more than just the two of you right from the beginning. Since it is a second marriage for at least one or both of you, the "fantasy" of marriage has been somewhat debunked. The reality of the situation is much clearer.

Don't even consider marrying that person who has children if you're not ready and willing to be a stepparent. It's a package deal. No matter how much you may love that person if you don't like children or if you don't like his or her children, don't enter into the marriage. You are making a choice—just like the choice of having your own child, adopting a child or becoming a foster parent. The fact that you have become a stepparent should not occur to you after-the-fact. No one would adopt a child without giving the decision a lot of thought beforehand. Loving someone, whether it be your spouse or children is not just a feeling, it is a conscious decision. It's more about what we do than about what we feel.

Remember love is patient and kind, it does not envy or boast, it is not proud, rude or seek its own way. It is not easily angered and it keeps no record of wrongs.

Love does not delight in evil but it rejoices with the truth. It always protects, always trusts, always hopes, and always prevails. Love never fails. (1 Cor. 13). These are actions not just feelings.

Love your spouse, love your children, and love your stepchildren, in the true sense of the word. You can be a stepparent-who is small-minded and holds a small place in the child's life.

Or you can be a Step   parent who takes too many steps back and keeps too big of a distance between yourself and the children, or aStep

                              parent who puts yourself above the family, or

        parent who puts yourself below the family
Step-

Be a STEPPARENT- big in the life of the child. Have a BIG impact by taking the high road.

How do you want to be remembered? The kind of stepparent you choose to be will not only impact the family now but also could determine the kind of relationship you will have with the children should anything happen to

74

your spouse. Should you fail to develop a healthy, loving relationship with your stepchild while your spouse is alive you may never see them again should your spouse die.

The stepparent may have all of the responsibilities of a parent but none of the rights. For example, under the FMLA (family medical leave act) the stepmother may take as long as a month off of work to care for a sick stepchild but she cannot sign a permission for treatment in a doctor's office or an emergency room. She would need, in writing, permission from both biological parents. She has no legal right to discuss the child's progress with a teacher.

The federal government allows individual states to determine the laws pertaining to marriage, divorce, and child custody. However, in most states stepparents have no legal guardianship of children under the age of eighteen. The biological parents are the only adults who can assume that role, even if one of the biological parents has been out of the picture and the stepparent has been "the Mom" or "the Dad" for most of the child's life. The courts define stepparents as "legal strangers" in the child's life.

Stepparents have a legal connection via the parent's remarriage but have no authority. Should the biological parent die the stepparent still has no rights.

So in the case of Cinderella, when her father died leaving her with an evil stepmother and stepsisters she would not have been left to live with them as a servant, she would have probably been put into foster care or an orphanage and that would have been another story.

With over 1/3 of the families in the U.S. being step families the courts are looking at these situations on a case-by-case basis. With so many blended families this has stepparent can show that a "bond was formed" they may be able to attain custody or visitation rights. The only way a stepparent may acquire legal custody of their stepchild is through the adoption process. This is a court-ordered process that terminates the rights of the biological parent not married to the stepparent. This is a process that must be agreed upon by both biological parents and the adoptive stepparent. When this occurs the child is still considered a stepchild, but the stepparent and their spouse now hold parental rights. (About Stepchildren by J. Paventi).

If a divorced mother has legal custody of a child, should she die, custody of the child immediately reverts to the biological father. I can only hope that, should my husband precede me in death, I have developed a close enough relationship with my stepchildren that they would maintain contact with me. I don't want to be a "legal stranger" in their lives; I want to be their friend, their stepmother. I have not done everything right. I keep trying, but I hope that some of the things I have observed and learned may help you in this most difficult but rewarding role. I have had no greater compliment than when my stepsons seek out my opinion or include me as one of the positive and significant people in their lives.

Perhaps this could all be summed up by asking you to imagine that you would become divorced or that you may precede your spouse in death and they were to remarry, bringing a stepparent into your children's lives. What kind of stepparent would you want your children to have?

That's the kind of stepparent you should be. My prayer is that these suggestions might make your job as a stepparent a little easier.

Do what you can to change the ending of your story. Don't let some handsome prince be the hero by taking your Cinderella out of a bad situation. Be the hero and live happily ever after as a family before he even arrives.

God Bless

Review of the 10 steps:

Stepping Stone #1-Don't try to become the other parent.

Stepping Stone #2-Speak positively about the other parent.

Stepping Stone #3-Do not compete.

Stepping Stone #4-Leave the disciplining to the natural parents.

Stepping Stone #5-Recognize the uniqueness of relationships.

Stepping Stone #6-Do not take frustrations with the ex-spouse out on the children.

Stepping Stone #7-Be aware of mixed messages.

Stepping Stone #8-Love your stepchildren like your own.

Stepping Stone #9-Remain in the background, take the supporting role.

Stepping Stone #10-Be the best stepparent this world has ever seen.

SECTION II

I would like to address those of you who find yourselves divorced and your ex-spouse has remarried, so your children now have a stepparent. The more I thought about the ten steps, I realized that these suggestions to the stepparent could also be helpful to those of you who have to deal with someone step-parenting your child. I know it can be an intimidating situation. You hate to think of anyone filling your role in your child's life. The stepping-stones from Section I, with some slight adjustments, may benefit you as well.

As the "real parent" you are a major player in your child's life. You have tremendous influence over the children and the situation. Your actions have the power to make a difficult situation either more difficult or considerably better for everyone involved, including yourself.

I realize that there are infinite scenarios that exist in

80

divorce and single parenting situations. I do not even begin to think that these suggestions will fit every situation. These are just general guidelines that may help you and your child weather the storm of divorce and come out the other end happier and healthier. The main idea behind the steps is to always consider what is best for the child, as well as getting over the hurt you have been through. Just because someone turned out to be a bad partner for you does not mean that they would make a bad parent. Try to have peace about your place in your child's life and allow your ex-spouse and his new partner their place as well.

Section II

Stones for the single, divorced parent

1-The new stepparent can never take your place.

2-Speak of the other parent and stepparent in positive terms.

3-Don't compete.

4-Be involved in the discipline of your child.

5-Build your own unique relationship with your child.

6-Don't take your frustrations with your ex-spouse out on the children.

7-Be aware of mixed messages.

8-Love your children.

9-Share and Be there.

10-Be the best parent you can be.

Stone #1-The new stepparent can never take your place.

The new stepparent is not your child's parent. You will always be the mother or father to your child, and no one can change that. Be the parent. Your ex-spouse's new partner cannot take your place. You don't need to feel threatened or feel the need to compete with the stepparent. You need only to continue filling the parental role that you have been given naturally.

The stepparent will be another influential adult in your child's life. If you stop to think about it there will always be additional, influential, important adults in your child's life. There will be many adults who will have a parental type role with your child. Your child may come to love and respect a teacher, a coach, a neighbor or a Sunday school teacher who is significant to them. Many people will make an impression along the way. You don't need to feel threatened or compete with them for position.

If your child is going to have a stepparent wouldn't you prefer it be someone who was kind? Someone they enjoy being around? Initially you may derive a small amount of satisfaction if your child doesn't like your ex's new partner. But how terrible for your child to spend every other weekend and holidays with someone they don't like.

If your child should come to love and respect the step-mom or step-dad, it's OK because no one can replace you. Relax, be proud that you have raised a child who has the capacity to love many people. One relationship can exist without infringing on another. Allow your child to love and respect all people don't discourage their ability to do that by competing with the stepparent and making your child feel torn between the two of you. You're all on the same team, there's no need for the child to chose sides.

Children suffer from anxiety, depression, migraines, acid reflux, and much more. There are many times when anxiety over family issues cause children to experience physical symptoms.

Children shouldn't have to worry about where to sit or who to talk to or which way to face because the adults in their lives can't get along. I've seen children react to situations like this by unconsciously acting out. They may do poorly in school, lie, wet the bed or exhibit any number of physical symptoms. Dad and Step Mom shouldn't make an issue over little Susie talking to Mom first after her concert! How great would it be for a child to feel at ease if their natural parents and their stepparents end up in the same room together during a special occasion or holiday.

Stone #2-Speak of the other parent and stepparent in positive terms.

Don't degrade yourself by speaking negatively about the other parent or the stepparent. It will only make you look bad to the child. You wouldn't think of bad mouthing a teacher or a coach who your child had come to love and respect; so there should be no reason to speak negatively about "the other parent" or stepparent who your child loves. We teach our children not to be nasty to people, therefore, we really can't justify our nastiness. Your child will learn a tremendous lesson about respect by observing the adults in their life. They are watching, at every age. As children of divorce grow into adulthood they will learn about relationships for themselves. They will see their parents as real people soon enough, "warts and all", and come to understand what led to the failure of their parents' marriage. Little needs to be said. Your children will come to have the utmost respect for you when they become adults and think back and realize that they have never heard you speak negatively about their stepparent or their other parent.

Hopefully they will never have to suffer through a divorce themselves but should they find themselves in that situation, with children involved, they will follow your example and handle it with dignity. It will also give them the hope that should they find themselves in a divorce situation they will be encouraged to know that it doesn't have to be ugly, filled with backstabbing and undermining. They can believe in a happily ever after divorce because they've seen you do it.

Should your ex-spouse or the stepparent not respond in kind, how much better are you going to look in your child's eyes by being the one who never speaks negatively of them?

Stone #3 You have no need to compete with the stepparent or with the other parent.

There is no contest for who is the best parent. If you're the Mom you shouldn't have to be the Dad, and if you're the Dad you shouldn't have to be the Mom. That's like trying to ask a bird to be a fish. The roles are completely different. Your role is secure, therefore there is no need to compete with the other parent or the stepparent. Children learn different things from each parent.

Being divorced is actually better than being a single parent due to the death or absence of the other parent. When one parent dies or is completely absent the remaining parent does have to fulfill the duties of both parents, which is unnatural and difficult. Children need both a Mom and a Dad. And although they may be divorced the child still has a Mom and a Dad, unless someone stands in the way.

Mother-daughter: much has been written about the Mother's role in raising a daughter. She is her daughter's role model. The mother directly and indirectly teaches her child about the woman's role in the world, in marriage and in mothering. A daughter learns by example that the woman is the nurturer, the heart of the family. She learns how to raise a child and how to be a spouse. A mother should show her daughter how to be a woman of substance, a woman with a peaceful and joyful spirit, even in the event of a divorce, not an angry and bitter woman.

Mother-son: a mother's role is to teach her son how to be a loving husband.
Her goal should be for him to become a man who is thoughtful and respectful of women.

Father-daughter: a father exemplifies to his daughter what to expect from her future husband. He is the example of what a man brings to the family as husband and father.

Father-son: a father teaches his son how to be a man of integrity how to be the head of the household without abusing his role of leadership. He is the example of how a husband should treat his wife and how a father treats his children.

Children need what each parent brings to the table, whether the parents are together or not, do not discount your child's need for the influence of the other parent.

Unless your child's other parent is completely out of the picture you only need to concern yourself with fulfilling your singular parental role. If you are a mother, just be the mother. It is next to impossible for a mother to fill a father's shoes, and vice versa. It's unnatural.

Granted not all parents are model parents but there still remains in all of us a need to have a relationship with our natural parents, regardless of the quality of their parenting. No one, not even you should become a roadblock to that. You have the right to choose not to continue in a relationship with someone but you do not have the right to decide that for your child.

I understand that due to circumstances that led to the divorce it is sometimes tempting to want to cut the other parent out of the picture but I would advise against it. It is cruel and selfish. If the other parent is failing to fulfill their role, you are not responsible for that as long as you are not the reason for it. So my advice is don't cut them out of your child's life and don't compete. It's not a competition it's a relationship.

Stone #4-You are the parent, so be involved in the discipline of your child.

When you see your children for such a limited time it is very difficult to be the disciplinarian, but you can't forfeit your responsibilities of being a parent. Just because you are divorced doesn't mean that you should become the child's friend instead of being the parent.

I'm sure it is tempting to fill the time you have with your child with just the fun stuff. When it is always in the children's best interest when the parents, together or not, are in agreement when it comes to discipline. You need to present a united front. You and your ex-spouse will always have the bond of the children so it is beneficial for everyone involved to communicate civilly. Sit down and discuss issues about how old your daughter should be to wear make-up or date. Agree together what the punishment should be for failing a class or missing a curfew. If the other parent is unwilling to work with you or fulfill their role as a disciplinarian and chooses instead to become "the friend" or the "cool parent" then you must be willing to remain the disciplinarian and do what you know is right.

Stone #5-Build your own unique relationship with your child.

The relationship you have with your son or daughter will go through the normal conflicts that go along with having a son or a daughter. Understand that conflicts are natural and don't blame your ex-spouse or the stepparent. As a Mom if you feel some competition with your daughter it may not be because the stepmom is interfering, it may be a natural phenomena. Daughters unknowingly compete with their mothers at times in their lives.

If you are a father with a son don't assume your ex-wife is encouraging your son to challenge you. He may be expressing his natural need to compete with you man to man.

It is also important not to exploit the natural tendencies that go along with the sexes of your children. For example, if you have a son and he is protective of you as the Mom don't exploit that and become a needy Mom. Dad, if you have a daughter who is especially close to you don't allow her to become so dependent on you that she is unable to grow into an independent woman. I have known women who where so emotionally dependent on their mothers or fathers that they were unable or unwilling to move away from them should their life with their husband require it. We are to leave our father and mother and cleave unto our husband. It is one of life's "necessary losses". (Judith Voist). Don't raise children who are emotional cripples, who are dependent on you into their adulthood just to fulfill your own emotional needs.

The relationship you build with your child is yours and yours alone. But make it a healthy one. Take the time to build it and don't use your ex-spouse or a stepparent as an excuse for your parent-child relationship shortcomings.

93

Relationships take time and attention. Devote both.

Stone #6-Don't take yourfrustrations with your ex-spouse out on the children.

Children need to be children. Children don't need to hear of or be part of conversations about adult issues. If there are child support issues involving medical needs or college, work it out between yourselves.

All children have physical needs that cost money. It is both parents responsibility to meet those needs and not necessarily the responsibility of the stepparent.

If the stepparent should choose to contribute financially to the needs of the children, that would be generous and helpful to both parents, but the stepparent is under no legal obligation to pay for the food, clothing, or shelter necessary to raise your child. If parents would remember this it would save the courts a lot of time and trouble.

Divorce ends your obligation to your spouse not to your children.

Don't make the child the go-between. Don't communicate through the child by saying the words, "You tell your father.......". Suck it up and call the other parent when necessary. The child didn't cause the divorce, and they are not little lawyers so they should not have to be the negotiators or the informers in the relationship.

Stone #7- Be aware of mixed messages.

Understand that your child has to live in two different homes. Although your differences caused enough conflict to create two separate homes where there was once just one, and the homes may have very different personalities, be respectful of the differences.

If you are a person who lives loosely and doesn't require a set schedule at least be respectful when a time or agreement has been established. If you are supposed to drop the children off fed and bathed by six o'clock, drop them off fed and bathed by six o'clock. If your ex feels the need to live by a schedule, help the child to understand that people have different ways of running their households. Not good or bad just different.

People divorce so that they can live their lives on their own terms. Children however don't get that freedom, they must live between two adults who have chosen to go in separate directions and who may live very different lifestyles.

Don't make a difficult situation even more difficult. By being critical, by messing with the schedules, by messing with the holidays just to mess with your ex—spouse. It will just mess up the child, by making them pawns. If you want your way of life to be respected then you need to respect your ex-spouse's way of life whether you agree with it or not.

Your children are living in two different homes with

two different sets of rules. Understand how confusing and frustrating this would be to anyone, especially to a child. Rules such as bedtime, bathing, mealtime, chores etc. will differ and may even completely contradict each other from home to home. I am not saying that you need to adjust your way of doing things or your parenting style according to your ex-spouse's style. But I am suggesting that you look at it from your child's perspective. Be understanding of the fact that this child moves back and forth in two worlds that aren't always in sync. You have a responsibility to make the situation, which you (not your child) created, run a little smoother. You may not be able to prevent conflicting messages due to personal differences but you need to understand that the child is receiving them.

If the child is struggling with dramatic differences and you find out the other parent allowed the child to do something that you disapprove of, don't blame the child. Discuss it, with your ex and then with your child, even if you cannot agree with your ex.

97

Yes, they need to follow the rules of your home but keep it in perspective by, remembering you can only control what takes place under your roof and on your watch. You never have control over another person's actions, even though it may affect your children. Unfortunately, divorce means that you no longer have a say in what your child's other parent does. This may be a very difficult situation to accept at times when you do not approve of the other parent's method of parenting, but it is better for you to keep your head and show your child another way of doing things so that when he/she is older they will judge for himself which is better. There may even be times where you feel that that other parents' style is putting your child in danger. If they are left alone at an earlier age than you would leave them or if they are permitted to drink or entertain themselves in a way that is not what you would consider age appropriate, you must discuss this with the other parent and hopefully reach some compromises. You may even lose some of the battles but you do not have to involve the child in the controversy if you are unsuccessful at resolving the controversy with your ex-spouse.

Stepping Stone #8-Love your children

I don't have to tell you to love your child as your own because they are your own. But I would say, don't ever stop loving them. The love chapter in the Bible, previously quoted states that love is patient, kind, humble, unselfish and not rude. These are the best guidelines of how to love someone but what is unspoken in these verses is that it is present. Love is being described as a way to act when you are in a relationship. In order to be in a relationship with your child you must be present. Being there is addressed further in the next "stone" in more detail.

Therefore, loving your child means that you are first and foremost in relationship with them. Loving them means that you will be patient with them, their other parent and stepparent. You will be kind, humble, unselfish and not rude to them, to their other parent and to their stepparent.

Loving your child means that you will continue in the responsibility of raising them. Raising them involves teaching them, disciplining them and helping them to grow into their full potential as an adult. Loving them involves the *work* of parenting.

Stone # 9-Share the important days in the child's life, BE THERE.

Statistics have shown that ten years after divorce, fathers will be entirely absent from the lives of 2/3 of children. If you find yourself single and your ex-spouse remarries don't attempt to cut the other parent out of your child's life because he has a "new family".

They will always need you both. So be at the concert or the ballgame or the play. Don't disappear. Even if you are a Dad who has only been given the right to see your children one day a week and every other weekend, reserve those days and weekends for your children. Yes, you have the right to get on with your life after divorce but don't ignore the responsibilities you had before the divorce.

I know of a man whose ex-wife, through manipulation of the system had prevented her children's father from ever seeing them. I'm sure it is very tempting in a situation like that to just want to get on with your life and start over but never forget what you are leaving behind.

Starting over and getting on with your life does not mean ignoring your previous responsibilities. Single after divorce is not the same as single before you were ever married with children. Those children still need you, probably more then ever. I would encourage estranged parents to fight the fight. Even if years go by, to the point of not seeing your children until they are grown and can seek you out on their own, be available. Even adult children want parents in their lives. Don't become just an acquaintance to your own child.

After divorce you have the desire and the need to rebuild your life but don't do it at the expense of your relationship with your child. Many parents just disappear, start over and leave the former children behind. You may no longer be a family but they are still your children. You deserve to be there.

When my daughters' graduated from high school and college, we were all there; me, my ex-husband, and his wife. On my daughters' wedding days we were all there. We were all there for the surprise 30th birthday party I had for my youngest daughter. I want their memories to include all of us.

There have been weddings where the mother has refused to attend if her ex-husband's new wife was also going to be there. Don't be ridiculous! These are once in a lifetime occasions. Don't cut off your nose to spite your face. If you think by missing special occasions because the stepparent is going to be there you will be making some kind of point, the only point you will make is that you are a bitter, petty person. You will be miserable and you will put a damper on some of the most important days of your child's life. So be there, take your rightful place and smile! It would also be very gracious of you if you also acknowledged the other parent and stepparent's desire to be there as well.

If you don't want to be invisible on those days neither does the stepparent. I guess the best way to explain how you should deal with the situation of your child having a stepparent is to follow the tried and true method of putting yourself in the other person's shoes. If you have not remarried, imagine that you had or will and you had acquired some stepchildren in the process. Treat the stepparent the way you would want to be treated.

A modern day approach to an old adage: Do unto others....... Not as they do unto you but as you would have them do unto you.

Stone #10-Be the best parent you can be. This is done by being the best person you can be.

Just because your marriage failed does not mean that you have failed as a parent. That child needs you more than ever. As a matter of fact because your child is now from a broken home it is more important than ever that you be a, loving, selfless parent, a stable anchor in their lives.

One who will set boundaries by disciplining and setting a good example of what a parent should be. You don't need to be seen by your child as the victim. Be a survivor. If you are an example to them that you can come out of divorce without anger and bitterness then they may also survive the divorce without anger and bitterness. If they see you being petty and vindictive towards their other parent and stepparent they will have a much more difficult time handling the divorce. If they see you happy and making the most of a difficult situation they will have less stress in their lives, and adopt your attitude. It's impossible for a divorce not to affect a child, but how you handle it can minimize the damage.

Think how much a child would benefit from having parents who are striving to be the best parent this world has ever seen as well as a stepparent trying to be the best stepparent as well. Although we will all fall short of that goal, it is a worthy one that even when we fall short we all still come out ahead.

Make the best of a bad situation, even if you must put your own feelings aside at times. Your child is worth the effort and you will all reap the benefits.

LIVE HAPPILY EVER AFTER
THE END.

Vignettes

Let's look at some situations encountered by a stepparent that, depending on how it's handled, could cause harm or help.

Prom Night-Tim and Tina were in their early forties. Tim had a 16 year-old daughter whom he had brought into his second marriage to Tina. His daughter, Ellie spent equal time with her biological parents. He mother had not remarried, so when Ellie was with her father and stepmother, her mother was alone. When Ellie's prom came up her stepmother offered to take her to look for a dress. This was a kind gesture in Tina's part and she felt that she was somewhat entitled since she and Tim were paying for the dress. Ellie's mother was not happy. She was already resenting that Ellie's prom fell on Tim and Tina's week-end and now she was not even to be a part of picking the dress. Tim saw no problem with any of this since it was only her prom, not her wedding and it was only a dress. Ellie felt torn. She appreciated that her Dad and stepmom were buying her a prom dress, and she normally enjoyed shopping with Tina but she felt terribly guilty that her Mom was not included.

Ellie couldn't really invite her Mom to go along, because she knew that this would have been awkward for everyone. What to do?

There is no right answer to the problem. There are many different ways the adults could handle this situation. First, Tina could have tried to put herself in Ellie's Mom's place and realized that it would be hard to be excluded from this event. Although she and Tim were paying for the dress she could have let Ellie and her Mom shop for it. Ellie's Mom would have been a part of the occasion and they (Tim and Tina) could have shared in the prom preparation and picture-taking portion of the evening.

Second, Ellie's Mom could have appreciated the fact that Tim and Tina were going to pay for the dress (thus relieving her of the financial burden) and let Tina shop with Ellie. Mom could have then asked if she could be there to take pictures as Ellie left for the prom with her date, therefore not feeling left out.

Third, however the arrangements of shopping and dressing for the prom were decided, the adults should discuss it amongst themselves, relieving Ellie of the guilt and powerlessness she felt worrying that someone will be hurt, which would put a cloud over her entire night.

Christmas-Zoe's parents divorce when she was only 5 years-old. Her father remarried when she was 15 and her mother dies when she was 25. Zoe was married and had two small children of her own. The woman that Zoe's father married had two sons who were also married and had children. Zoe wouldn't really say that she didn't get along with her stepmother, they were cordial to each other but she didn't feel exceptionally close to her. It's not that

Zoe didn't want a relationship with her it was just that Zoe felt that her stepmother always kept her at arms length. Her stepmother and her mother never got along and her stepmother knew that Zoe was close to her mother until the day she died. Holidays were difficult because her stepmother seemed to feel that her family consisted of her own two sons and Zoe's father. She never included Zoe and her family in holiday gatherings.

First, Zoe's father should speak up. He should let his new wife know that Zoe is his daughter, and her children are his grandchildren. Even before Zoe's mother's death he needed to include Zoe in his holiday plans. He should see that now more than ever with her mother gone she needs him more than ever.

Second, Zoe's stepmother needs to put aside any bad feelings or insecurities that she may have felt related to Zoe's mother. Zoe is not a threat to her, her marriage or her family. She has a wonderful opportunity to develop a close relationship with a "daughter". Her sons would have

109

the chance to have a sister that they never had as well as nieces and nephews and cousins for their children. Expanding our relationships enriches our lives it doesn't deplete them. She could help her husband to make up for time that he wasn't there for Zoe because of the divorce that occurred early in Zoe's life. An opportunity that I am sure he would thank her for. Including Zoe in her life would hurt no one and would help everyone. But she may need to put aside her own feelings long enough for the awkwardness to change into a comfortable new norm for their family. If the stepmother would initiate this it would only enrich her marriage. By taking this step it would also avoid any conflict that would occur if her husband were to insist or force the issue.

Yes, Zoe's father should have rectified the holiday situation when Zoe was still young. Had he made it clear to his new wife from the beginning that he was a package deal and that he had a daughter that was to be part of their family. he could have saved everyone years of hurt. But it is never too late to fix what has been broken. Who knows how many Christmases we have left.

R-rated movies- When Keith (17) was with his father he was allowed to watch R-rated movies. When he was with his mother and stepfather he wasn't. Now what?? This had become an issue that was causing arguments in both homes. Keith's Dad didn't want anyone to tell him what he should do in his own home. Keith's Mom was not about to let her son watch R-rate movies in her home. Keith's stepdad was in the middle. He wanted to support his wife. If he supported the no R-movies rule his stepson would be mad, if he stayed out of it completely and allowed his stepson to watch R-movies when his mother wasn't home he was putting himself in a position that could harm his marriage. He certainly had no control or influence over what Keith's father did or what his value system was.

First, Keith's parents should discuss the issue between themselves. If his mother cannot change his father's position on the issue, all that she can do is present her reasons and make clear her rules for her home.

Second, Keith's father should hear is son's mother's position and consider what is best for their son. Considering only what is the best approach for a 17 year-old boy and attempting to put aside any secondary motivation to use the issue against his ex-wife.

Third-If the parents cannot agree between themselves on the issue than each one must calmly explain to Keith their reasons for their rule and explain that different rules may exist in each home. When Keith is with his father he may watch things that his mother doesn't approve of but has no control over and when he is with his mother her may not watch things that he may have been able to watch at his father's house. The stepparent can only discuss it with Keith as an adult who will support his spouse in her decision and possibly be someone who Keith can discuss the pros and cons with objectively.

There is no need to argue about things that you can't

control. Each parent has the right to dictate what goes on in his or her home. The child will know the rules for each and is expected to respect each home's rules without argument. The stepparent need only support his spouse and be an adult who can be a resource for the child to discuss controversial subjects.

Little League Championship-Noah played baseball every week-end from April to June. Long games on Wednesday nights and every Saturday, with tournaments that could take up the entire week-end. Rachel was married to Noah's father and had a new baby. She hated the hours that these baseball games took her husband away. Her alternative was to drag an infant to hot dusty baseball games and sit on uncomfortable bleachers for hours. To top it all off if she did go along she would be confronted with her husband's ex-wife and her husband. Her dilemma had many sides. Give up her week-ends with her husband, sit at a hot dusty field with a baby, try to avoid completely or make conversation with her husband's ex-wife or stay home by herself for hours.

COMPROMISE. First-Rachel would have had some of the same issues to deal with if Noah were her own son. The games still take hours, in the heat and dust and her husband would still want to be there.

Second- if she did chose to go she should do it happily. Maybe not going to every game but going to show Noah that she cared to see him play.

Third-When she chooses not to go, she can allow her husband to go without consequences. It is his son and he should be there. If Noah were her own son there may be times when her husband would go to a game and she would stay home with the baby. She shouldn't resent his time away for his child.

Fourth-Should Noah's mother and her husband be there, don't resent it. They belong there too. It is nothing but good for a child to see all involved in his life showing an interest in his activities. It is great for him to see his parents at the same place at the same time without incident. There are too many possible scenarios to try to cover. But they all have one thing in common. Whether you are the parent or the stepparent, put aside your own feelings and do what is best for the child/children. You will reap the benefits in the end.